EILEEN DIAMOND
LET'S MAKE MUSIC FUN!
THE GREEN SONGBOOK

Introduction

In this volume of **Let's Make Music Fun!** Eileen Diamond has included a colourful selection of familiar and new songs including action songs, part songs, story songs, instrumental songs and rounds, to form a unique library of topical source material for pre-school, Key Stage one and Key Stage two.

Each song is provided with teaching ideas and notes on performance which help to explore and satisfy a whole range of National Curriculum requirements.

To help find the material you require, all songs have been identified by Key Stage and song type. Piano accompaniments have been simplified and chord symbols have been added.

Children will enjoy singing these catchy songs over and over again. Fun to learn and fun to teach!

Credits

Music and text processed by Halstan & Co. Ltd., Amersham, Bucks., England and
Crabtree Music, PO Box 484, Bury St. Edmunds, Suffolk, England
Vocals on recording: Niki Davies and Michael Winsor
Recordings orchestrated and engineered by Dave Corbett
Cover design by Glide Design

Published 1997

International
MUSIC
Publications

Contents

Alphabetical Song Listing

Learning A Round

Each round should be learnt in unison before part singing is attempted. The instrumentation listed for the rounds is only a suggestion and may be varied according to which instruments are available at the time. Although melody instruments and not used in these arrangements, there is no reason why recorders, strings and other 'c' instruments should not be included. If a selection of several rounds are performed in a concert, vary the instrumentation.

Any of the INSTRUMENTAL or VOICE parts may be omitted from the OSTINATO. The rounds may also be sung unaccompanied, in which case it will be necessary to play a starting note. A useful performance plan is as follows:

1. PIANO plays 4 bars OSTINATO once (or 2 bars twice) alone.
2. PERCUSSION INSTRUMENTS join in OSTINATO in turn.
3. VOICES join in the OSTINATO and continue into the round. The round is sung once in unison, then three times in parts.

Key

(A)   Action Song

(I)   Instrumental Song

(R)   Round

(P)   Part Song

(S)   Song just for singing

(P▽)   Material suitable for pre-school.

(1▽)   Material suitable for key stage one.

(2▽)   Material suitable for key stage two.

Clothes

Words and Music by
Eileen Diamond

Performance   Accomp.

Playfully, with a swing

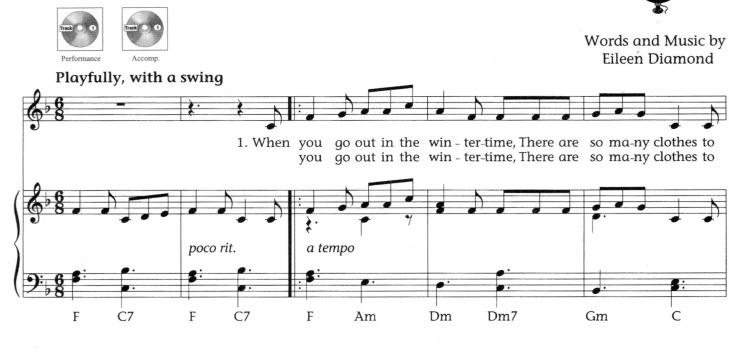

1. When you go out in the win-ter-time, There are so ma-ny clothes to
   you go out in the win-ter-time, There are so ma-ny clothes to

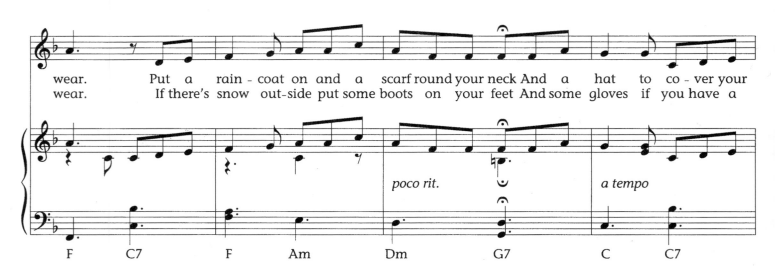

wear. Put a rain-coat on and a scarf round your neck And a hat to co-ver your
wear. If there's snow out-side put some boots on your feet And some gloves if you have a

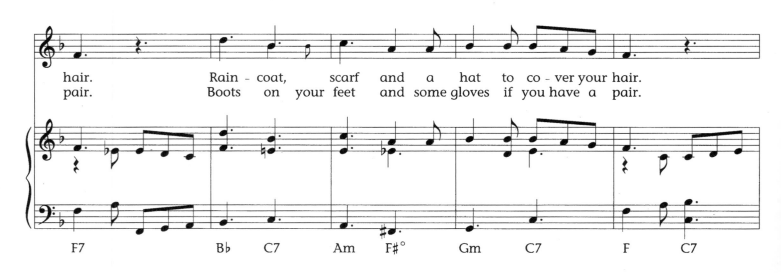

hair. Rain-coat, scarf and a hat to co-ver your hair.
pair. Boots on your feet and some gloves if you have a pair.

5

1. When you go out in the wintertime,
   There are so many clothes to wear.
   Put a raincoat on and a scarf round your neck
   And a hat to cover your hair.
   Raincoat, scarf and a hat to cover your hair.

2. When you go out in the wintertime,
   There are so many clothes to wear.
   If there's snow outside put some boots on your feet
   And some gloves if you have a pair.
   Boots on your feet and some gloves if you have a pair.

3. Out you go in the cold and rain,
   If you're well covered up you don't care.
   With your raincoat and scarf, boots and gloves
   And a hat to cover your hair.
   With your raincoat and scarf, boots and gloves
   And a hat to cover your hair.

TEACHING IDEAS

An action song which would link well with topics such as hot and cold, weather, seasons, fabrics etc.

Performance

The children mime the actions of putting on the various clothes. From the words 'Out you go' to 'Care', they walk around, then repeat the actions of putting on the clothes until the end, when they walk around again before sitting down at the final chord.

Further discussion and development ideas

Discuss how wearing many layers of clothing helps you to keep warm. How do animals keep warm in the winter? What kind of fabrics do we wear in cold weather and also in hot weather? Talk about some fabrics being waterproof to keep out the wet as well as the cold.

Rainbow

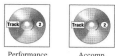

Words and Music by
Eileen Diamond

Gently, but not too fast

Do you know the col-ours of a rain-bow? Have you seen one stretched a-cross the sky? There are sev-en col-ours in a rain-bow, Can you name them? Let's try! There's red and or-ange and

F7 Bb Cm7 F7 Bb Eb Cm7 F7 Bb F7 Bb D7 Eb C7 F7 Bb D7

Do you know the colours of a rainbow?
Have you seen one stretched across the sky?
There are seven colours in a rainbow,
Can you name them? Let's try!

There's red and orange and yellow
There's green and blue,
The last two colours in the set,
Are indigo and violet.

Pretty rainbow, rainbow.
Through the rain and sun your colours glow,
Please don't go pretty rainbow.

TEACHING IDEAS

A song to tie in with weather and science topics which makes an attractive visual performance as well as holding the children's attention. It also helps them to learn the sequence of colours in a rainbow.

Performance

Learn it all together first then the children could divide into two groups. The first group sing as far as 'sky?' Then the second group sing up to 'Let's try'. Then group 1 take over again as far as 'blue' and group 2 continue up to 'violet' after which they all sing together to the end.

Further discussion and development ideas

For a concert performance cut out seven rainbow shapes from some stiff card and paint each one a different colour of the rainbow. Then cut out two more shapes and paint a complete rainbow on each.

Choose seven children to hold the rainbow colours in the right order and with the colour face to the audience. Then choose two more children to hold the complete rainbows, one at either end of the line of colours. As each colour is sung, the child holding that colour raises it above her/his head and keeps it there until the end of the song. When the words 'Pretty rainbow' are sung, the two children holding the rainbows at either end raise them too.

Busy Hands

Words and Music by
Eileen Diamond

1. Slap, clap, tap on your chest.
    Slap, clap, tap on your chest.
    Busy hands move up and down,
    Then start all over again.

2. Slap, clap, tap on your chest.
    Slap, clap, tap on your chest.
    Busy hands move up and down,
    Then fold them over to rest.

TEACHING IDEAS

A simple action song for the younger children, involving co-ordination with a strong rhythmic feel.

Performance

When the children are familiar with the song, try leaving out the words 'Slap, clap' and just do the actions. Following that, leave out the words 'Tap on your chest' as well and do the actions instead. Then just perform the actions to the music for the first half of the song and join in with the words from 'Busy hands...' to the end. This is fun to do as well as offering the children a secure sense of rhythm and encouraging concentration.

Slap, clap, tap on your chest *Slap, clap, tap on your chest*	Slap knees once, clap hands once, tap chest with alternate hands to rhythm of words.
Busy hands move up and down	Stretch hands up high and down again twice.
Then start all over again	Lay hands ready on lap.
Then fold them over to rest	Fold arms across chest.

Do What You Feel Like Doing

Words and Music by
Eileen Diamond

oth - ers know what's on your mind. It's good to let your

feel - ings go And leave your cares be - hind. 2. Give your feet a day.

1. Give a friendly wave if you want to,
   If that's what you feel like,
   Do what you feel like doing.

   Give a friendly wave if you want to,
   If that's what you feel like,
   Do what you feel like today.

CHORUS. It's good to let your feelings show,
So others know what's on your mind.
It's good to let your feelings go
And leave your cares behind.

2. Give your feet a stamp if you want to,
   If that's what you feel like,
   Do what you feel like doing.

   Give your feet a stamp if you want to,
   If that's what you feel like,
   Do what you feel like today.

TEACHING IDEAS

An imaginative song encouraging children to move rhythmically and expressively to music.

Performance

The children perform the actions indicated by the words.

There are many different actions that could be performed with this song such as:

Try to beat the time / Dance around the floor / Jump up in the air / March around the room

Further discussion and development ideas

After trying some of the suggested ideas, ask the children what *they* feel like doing and use their ideas.

Let's All Play Along

Words and Music by
Eileen Diamond

Dav - id's play-ing on the drum, On the drum, on the drum. Dav - id's play-ing on the drum, On the drum, on the drum.

Let's all play a-long with Dav - id, With Dav - id, with

1. David's playing on the drum,
   On the drum, on the drum.
   David's playing on the drum,
   On the drum, on the drum.

   Let's all play along with David,
   With David, with David.
   Let's all play along with David,
   It's fun when we all play together in the band.

TEACHING IDEAS

A simple-to-perform percussion song for young children which helps them to feel a steady beat while playing along with their instruments. It also gives them the opportunity to learn to control their instruments by playing quietly when they play together and louder, though not harshly, when they play alone.

Performance

Any available percussion instruments may be used. Choose a few children to stand in front of the others, each with a different instrument and give the remaining children a selection of instruments to play.

The soloists take turns to play in the first half of the song and are joined by the rest of the class for 'Let's all play along'. Adapt the rhythm where necessary for different names and instruments.

Further discussion and development ideas

Experiment with different sound levels of play, with solo and ensemble instruments.

The Months Of The Year

Words and Music by
Eileen Diamond

Jan - u - ar - y, Feb - ru - ar - y, March and Ap - ril Are the first four months of the year. May, June, Ju - ly and Au - gust Show that sum - mer-time is here. Sep -

January, February, March and April
Are the first four months of the year.
May, June, July and August
Show that summertime is here.

September and October
When the leaves are falling fast,
Then November, followed by December,
Means that another year has passed.

TEACHING IDEAS

A useful and easy-to-remember way of teaching the months of the year.

Performance

The children may like to make a falling movement with their hands for 'When the leaves are falling fast'.

One Hand Here, One Hand There

Words and Music by
Eileen Diamond

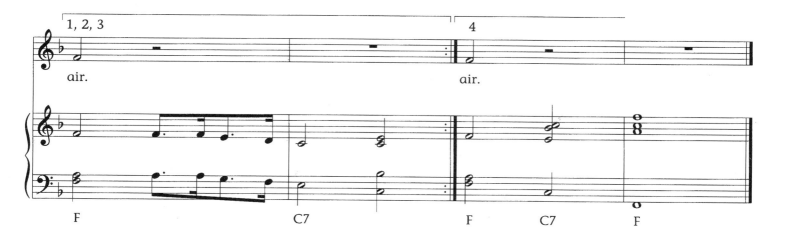

1. One hand here, one hand there,
   Left one, right one, clap them both together.
   One hand here, one hand there,
   One hand, two hands, clap them in the air,
   Clap them in the air, clap them in the air.

2. One thumb here, one thumb there,
   Left one, right one, twiddle them both together.
   One thumb here, one thumb there,
   One thumb, two thumbs, twiddle them in the air,
   Twiddle them in the air, twiddle them in the air.

3. One wrist here, one wrist there,
   Left one, right one, shake them both together. etc.

4. One arm here, one arm there,
   Left one, right one, wave them both together. etc.

 TEACHING IDEAS

An action song all about 'Left' and 'Right'.

Performance

The children perform the appropriate actions.

If you are performing opposite the children, remember to use opposite hands! For very young children, the words 'This one, that one' may be used if preferred, instead of 'Left one, right one'.

Sing When You're Happy

Words and Music by
Eileen Diamond

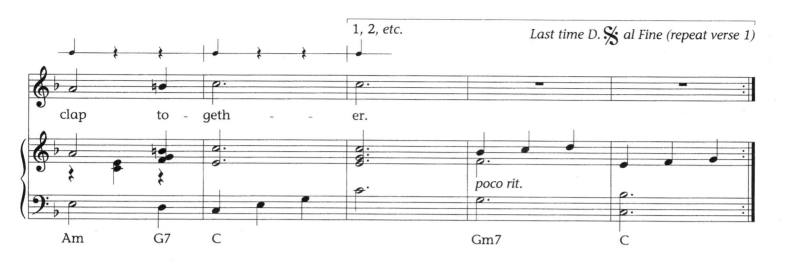

1. Sing when you're happy and clap your hands,
   Clap your hands, clap your hands.
   Sing when you're happy and clap your hands,
   Clap your hands like this.
   Sing la, la, la. Clap!
   Sing and clap together.

2. Sing when you're happy and slap your knees, etc.

3. Sing when you're happy and pat your head, etc.

4. Sing when you're happy and beat your fists, etc.

TEACHING IDEAS

A useful song for co-ordination of sound, action and memorising short musical patterns.

Performance

Verse 1. Clap your hands

Verse 2. Slap your knees

Verse 3. Pat your head

Verse 4. Beat your fists

Many actions can be used with this song. Ask the children for their ideas and use as many verses as wished.

Note the change of clapping pattern at the end of the verse when singing and clapping together. The clapping patterns may be learnt by ear or from symbols. For a change, percussion instruments may be used e.g.

Sing when you're happy and play the drum

Further discussion and development ideas

Try using different clapping rhythms e.g.

The children may like to make some up.

Things To Do

Words and Music by
Eileen Diamond

Stretching, stretching up 'til I'm tall,
Rolling, rolling down 'til I'm small.
Flying, flying like an aeroplane.
Jump up, turn around, sit down again.

 # TEACHING IDEAS

A song to encourage imaginative movement. The varied actions within this short and simple song, encourage participation by very young children and those with short attention spans.

Performance

Stretching, stretching up 'til I'm tall	Stretch up
Rolling, rolling down 'til I'm small	Roll hands around while bending down
Flying, flying like an aeroplane	Stretch arms out to the side and move them up and down
Jump up, turn around	Jump up, turn around
Sit down again	Sit down

Two

Words and Music by
Eileen Diamond

Happily

CHORUS Doo-dl-y doo de doo de doo de doo de doo,

Doo-dl-y doo de doo de doo de doo de doo.

1. Two feet to take you walk-ing, Two feet to move you a-round,

CHORUS Doodly doo de doo de doo de doo de doo,
Doodly doo de doo de doo de doo de doo.

1. Two feet to take you walking,
Two feet to move you around,
Two feet when you feel like dancing,
Two feet to jump off the ground.
CHORUS

2. Two eyes to read a book with,
Two eyes to look all around,
Two eyes when you go out searching,
Two eyes to see what you've found.
CHORUS

3. Two hands to do up buttons,
Two hands to pull on a hat,
Two hands you can catch a ball with,
Two hands for holding a bat.
CHORUS

4. Two arms to swim in the water,
Two arms to stretch in the air,
Two arms you can wrap round someone,
Two arms to show that you care.

Doodly doo de doo de doo de doo de doo,
Doodly doo de doo de doo de doo de doo.
Doodly doo de doo de doo doo,
Doo, doo, doo,
Doodly doo, doo doo!

TEACHING IDEAS

A song to encourage imaginative movements to music and suitable for body topics.

Performance

It's useful to teach the 'Doodly doo' chorus first to keep the song going in between the actions.

The children perform appropriate actions while singing the verse and gently sway their bodies in time to the chorus.

Further discussion and development ideas

Talk about other parts of the body that come in twos.

Feet

Words and Music by
Eileen Diamond

Jauntily

CHORUS

There are feet for walk-ing and feet for stalk-ing, And feet for swim-ming and feet for cling-ing, And feet for hop-ping, __ feet clip clop-ping down the street, What a lot of diff-erent feet! There are feet for walk-ing and feet for stalk-ing, And feet for swim-ming and feet for cling-ing, And feet for hop-ping, __ feet clip clop-ping down the

Last verse to Coda

CHORUS. There are feet for walking and feet for stalking,
And feet for swimming and feet for clinging,
And feet for hopping, feet clip clopping down the street,
What a lot of different feet!

There are feet for walking and feet for stalking,
And feet for swimming and feet for clinging,
And feet for hopping, feet for clip clopping down the street.

1. The feet of a lion you can see,
Are soft and padded for stalking,
Then take a look at the feet of a man,
There are heels and toes for walking.

   CHORUS

2. The feet of a duck are flat and webbed,
This makes them good for swimming,
Then take a look at the feet of a bat,
They are specially shaped for clinging.

   CHORUS

3. The feet of a horse go clippetty clop,
When he takes people out riding,
A snake doesn't have any feet at all,
So he can only go sliding.

   CHORUS
   What a lot of feet!

TEACHING IDEAS

A fun song with a catchy chorus and topical interest.

Performance

Walking, stalking, swimming, clinging, hopping, clip-clopping . . . !

Further discussion and development ideas

What a lot of different feet! Try to find pictures of the feet of the different animals mentioned in this song. Also, ask the children if they can name some other animals that have webbed feet, padded feet, hooves etc.

We Will Hear A Rhythm

Words and Music by
Eileen Diamond

Steadily, not too fast

Lyrics:

We will hear a rhythm on the pia - no, Listen to it ve - ry care - ful - ly. We will hear a rhythm on the pia - no, See if you can clap / play it af - ter me.

We will hear a rhythm on the piano,
Listen to it very carefully.
We will hear a rhythm on the piano,
See if you can clap ⎱ it after me.
             play ⎰

 TEACHING IDEAS

A song to encourage the ability to recall and imitate a short rhythmic pattern. It is also useful for introducing rhythmic improvisation.

Performance

Set out a number of different percussion instruments such as; DRUM, TAMBOURINE, CLAVES, WOOD BLOCK, TRIANGLE, CHIME BAR.

Everyone sings the first six bars then the teacher sings 'See if you can clap it after me'.

The teacher then plays a short rhythmic pattern on one note and the children clap it afterwards.

Next, the teacher chooses two children and they each select an instrument. After the song is repeated, the first child sings (or says) "See if you can play it after me" and proceeds to play a rhythm. The second child copies the rhythm on his/her instrument, then while the first child sits down, the second child chooses a successor to play a rhythm that she/he will make up after the song is repeated again and so on.

At each repetition, the words of the song are changed to correspond with the instrument being used.

e.g. We will hear a rhythm on the tam - bour - ine. *etc.*

When all the instruments have been used, the last child sings "See if you can clap it after me" and the remaining children clap the rhythm.

Further discussion and development ideas

For older children, this song could be used for melodic as well as rhythmic improvisation by singing: 'We will hear a tune upon the xylophone' or 'We will hear a tune on the recorder' and then 'See if you can sing it after me'. Any tuned instrument may be used.

Choose An Instrument

Words and Music by
Eileen Diamond

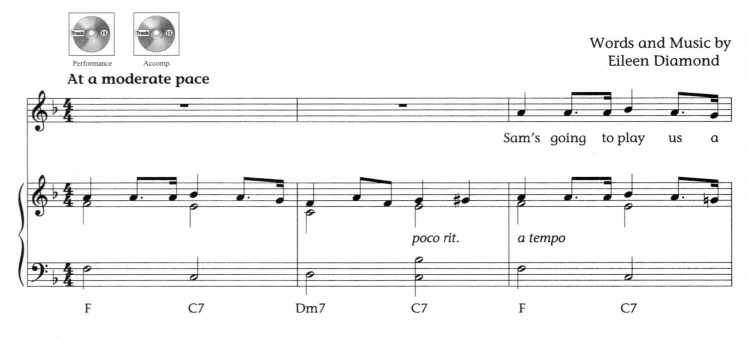

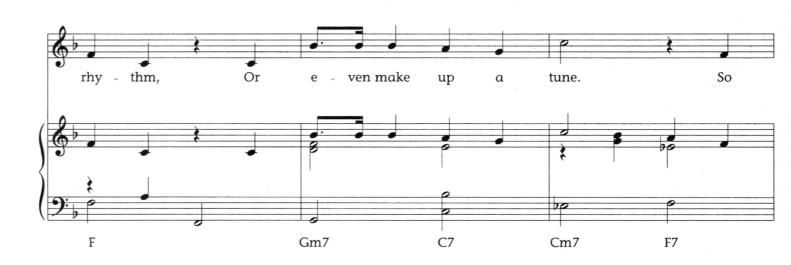

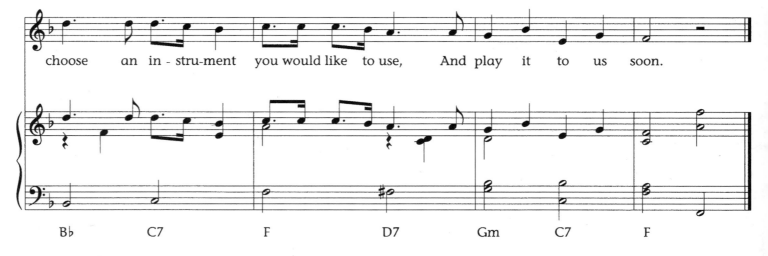

Sam's going to play us a rhythm,
Or even make up a tune.
So choose an instrument you would like to use,
And play it to us soon.

  # TEACHING IDEAS

A song to encourage both rhythmic and melody improvisation as well as listening skills.

Performance

The children take turns at choosing either an untuned or a tuned percussion instrument on which to make up a short rhythm or melody after singing the song. The other children then clap the rhythm, or sing the melody after listening to it.

The following instruments may be suitable:

TUNED

Xylophone, metallophone, glockenspiel
piano, recorder, chime bars, or any other
instrument the children are able to play.

UNTUNED

Claves, drum, wood block,
tambourine

Further discussion and development ideas

The children may like to try working in pairs with one child making up the first half of a melody and the other child making up an answering phrase to finish it off. Similarly, this may be done with the children making up rhythms on untuned instruments.

Mr McGrew

Words and Music by
Eileen Diamond

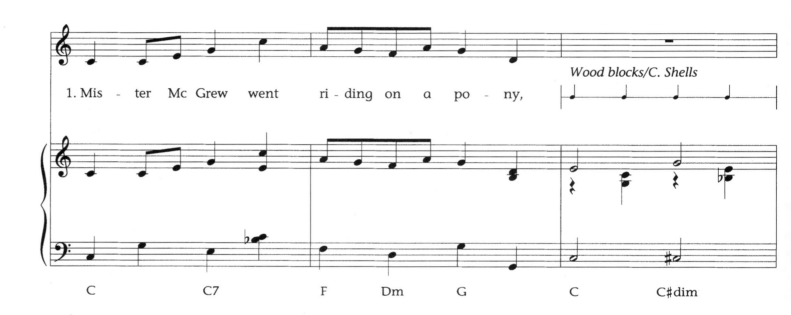

1. Mis - ter Mc Grew went ri - ding on a po - ny,

Wood blocks/C. Shells

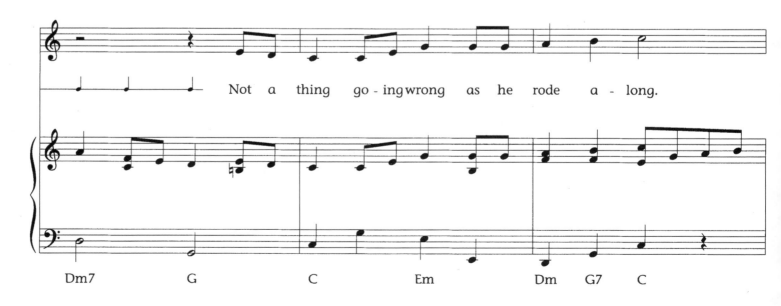

Not a thing go - ing wrong as he rode a - long.

1. Mister McGrew went riding on a pony,
   Not a thing going wrong as he rode along.

2. Then all at once he heard a clap of thunder,
   And the thunder made a sound that echoed all around,
   But Mister McGrew kept riding on his pony.

3. It grew very dark and down came the rain.
   And the rain made a sound that echoed all around,
   After the thunder;
   But Mister McGrew kept riding on his pony.

4. Then after a while, the wind began to blow.
   And the wind made a sound that echoed all around,
   After the rain came,after the thunder;
   But Mister McGrew kept riding on his pony.

5. A truck passed him by and hooted on his horn.
   And the truck made a sound that echoed all around,
   After the wind blew, after the rain came, after the thunder;
   But Mister McGrew kept riding his pony.

6. A bee buzzed around and stung him on the nose.
   And the bee made a sound that echoed all around,
   After the truck passed, after the wind blew, after the rain came, after the thunder;

TEACHING IDEAS

A song using percussion instruments to depict sounds that occur in the story. The song may also be performed using actions and body sounds instead of instruments, or with a combination of both . . . see below. The song is accumulative; each verse adding a different instrument. This holds the children's attention as they wait for the right moment to play. The steady clip-clop of the coconut shells helps the children to feel and maintain a regular beat.

Performance

	INSTRUMENTS	ACTIONS
PONY	WOOD BLOCKS/COCONUT SHELLS	Tongue clicking
THUNDER	CYMBALS	Feet stamping
RAIN	TAMBOURINES	Knee slapping
WIND	GLOCKENSPIELS/XYLOPHONES/ METALLOPHONES/GLISSANDI (sliding up and down)	Blow/whistle
TRUCK	RECORDER (any note)	'Beep beep' sounds
BEE	SCRAPER	Buzzing sound

Discuss the story with the children and match up the sounds with the appropriate instruments. After distributing the instruments, re-tell the story with the children adding the sound effects.

The song is accumulative. After each new verse, the previous ones are added in the following way:

Verse 5   'After the wind blew' is followed by   Verse 6   After the truck passed,
           After the rain came,   After the wind blew,
           After the thunder,   After the rain came,
           But Mr Mc Grew kept riding on his pony   After the thunder
                                                                    But Mr Mc Grew kept riding on his pony

Further discussion and development ideas
Ask the children to make up their own story using percussion instruments to create sound effects.

Thanks

Words and Music by
Eileen Diamond

The 1. sun gives us warmth, the sun gives us light. It
2. air's all a - round to breathe in and out. We

shows us the dif - ference be - tween day and night. Thanks for the
must keep it heal - thy, that's what life's a - bout. Thanks for the

CHORUS

sun. Thanks for the sun.   For the sun in the sky and the
air. Thanks for the air.

air all a - round, For the plants that grow in the fer - tile ground, We're

1. The sun gives us warmth, the sun gives us light.
   It shows us the difference between day and night.
   Thanks for the sun. Thanks for the sun.

CHORUS.   For the sun in the sky and the air all around,
   For the plants that grow in the fertile ground,
   We're thankful every day. We're thankful every day.

2. The air's all around to breathe in and out.
   We must keep it healthy, that's what life's about.
   Thanks for the air. Thanks for the air.

   CHORUS

3. The plants give us food which helps us to grow,
   Our life wouldn't flourish without them we know.
   Thanks for the plants. Thanks for the plants.

 TEACHING IDEAS

A tuneful, thought provoking song to encourage environmental and social awareness which, without exemplifying any one religion, would be suitable for General Assembly.

Performance

Try singing the verses with a fairly quiet tone and then sing the CHORUS a little louder.

Further discussion and development ideas

Ask the children what other things they are especially thankful for.

On Christmas Day

Words and Music by
Eileen Diamond

Lyrics:

1. Ber - ries of red on hol - ly grow, Ber - ries of white on mis - tle - toe And
2. Jin - gl - ing bells and bells that chime, Ev - ery - one has a jol - ly time And

that's what you see on Christ-mas Day.
that's what you hear on Christ-mas Day. Put up dec - or - a - tions,

1. Berries of red on holly grow,
   Berries of white on Mistletoe
   And that's what you see on Christmas Day.

2. Jingling bells and bells that chime,
   Everyone has a jolly time
   And that's what you hear on Christmas Day.

   Put up decorations, lights and Christmas trees.
   Happy celebrations, happy families!
   It's the day to remember Jesus' birth,
   Friendship and love to all on earth
   And that's what you hope on Christmas Day.
   That's what you hope on Christmas Day.

TEACHING IDEAS

A merry sing-along Christmas song, with words encompassing the joyful aspects of Christmas.

Further discussion and development ideas

Ask the children for their ideas about the celebration of Christmas Day. What do they see? What do they hear? What do they hope?

I Can't Stop Tapping my Feet

Words and Music by
Eileen Diamond

Very lively

When you hear some mu-sic play-ing and it has a catch-y beat, And some-thing in the rhy-thm makes you want to tap your feet, Then your

When you hear some music playing and it has a catchy beat,
And something in the rhythm makes you want to tap your feet,
Then your fingers want to snap and your hands start to clap,
Oh this is quite outrageous, it's too contagious!
I can't stop, I can't stop moving.

1. I can't stop tapping my feet no, I can't stop tapping my feet
   No, I can't stop tapping my feet while the music's playing that beat.
   Tap, tappetty tap, tappetty tap, tappetty tap, tap.
   Tap, tappetty tap, tappetty tap, tappetty tap.

2. Oh, I can't stop snapping my fingers, etc.

3. Oh, I can't stop clapping my hands no, etc.

   Oh, I can't stop tapping my feet no, I can't stop tapping my feet
   No, I can't stop tapping my feet while the music's playing that beat.

 # TEACHING IDEAS

An easy-to-learn, very catchy action song for all ages.

Performance

Tap, snap and clap as directed in the song. Children will want to join in instantly and spontaneously with the repetitive catchy choruses combined with actions and true to its title, they will probably continue long after it's finished!

Have A Very
Merry Christmas Day

Words and Music by
Eileen Diamond

1. Christmas, Christmas,
    Snowflakes falling and children calling out
    Christmas, Christmas,
    Have a very merry Christmas Day.

    Christmas, Christmas,
    Church bells ringing and carol singing at
    Christmas, Christmas,
    Have a very merry Christmas Day!
    Have a Christmas full of good cheer,
    And a very happy new year,
    Have a very merry Christmas Day!

2. Christmas, Christmas,
    People shopping and present swapping at
    Christmas, Christmas,
    Have a very merry Christmas Day.

    Christmas, Christmas,
    Friendly faces in welcome places at
    Christmas, Christmas,
    Have a very merry Christmas Day!
    Have a day that's happy and bright,
    Full of gladness, joy and delight.
    Have a very merry Christmas Day!

 # TEACHING IDEAS

Type of song

A happy Christmas song for all ages and one which would make a good finale for a concert.

The Birthday Round
(3 part round)

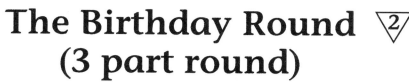

Joyfully

Words and Music by
Eileen Diamond

Accompaniment Ostinato

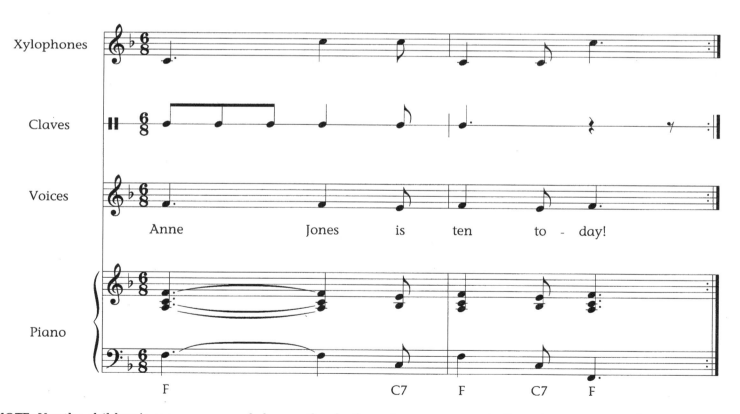

NOTE: Use the children's own names and change the rhythm where necessary to fit various names and ages.
(It may sometimes be necessary to use an up-beat).

It's Christmas Time Again

Words and Music by
Eileen Diamond

56

Group 1

1. Snowflakes falling on the ground outside,
   Christmas cards arrive from far and wide,
   Presents waiting to be wrapped and tied
   Because it's Christmas time again.

2. Twinkling lights upon the Christmas tree,
   Children singing carols merrily,
   Hanging mistletoe for all to see
   Because it's Christmas time again.

3. Ding dong ding dong ding.
   Ding dong ding, let everybody sing,
   And there'll be hot roast turkey and a pudding after,
   Jokes and paper hats and sounds of laughter,
   Streamers hanging from a paper chain
   Because it's Christmas time, it's Christmas time
   It's Christmas time again

Group 2

1. Snowflakes falling on the ground outside,
   Christmas cards arrive from far and wide,
   Presents waiting
   'Cause it's Christmas time again.

2. Twinkling lights upon the Christmas tree,
   Children singing carols merrily.
   Hanging mistletoe,
   It's Christmas time again.

3. Ding dong ding dong, ring out the church bells,
   Ding dong ding, let everybody sing,
   Hot roast turkey and a pudding after,
   Jokes and paper hats and sounds of laughter,
   Paper chain
   Because it's Christmas time, it's Christmas time,
   It's Christmas time again.

TEACHING NOTES

An effective two-part song for the older children.

Performance
Make sure each part is listened to and learnt securely first on its own before attempting them together.

Frost And Snow
(Four part round)

Words and Music by
Eileen Diamond

Performance   Accomp.

Moderately

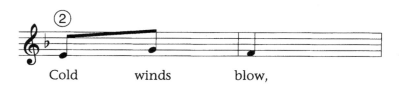

Frost   and   snow

Cold   winds   blow,

Fires   a - glow   It's

Win - ter   time.

Accompaniment Ostinato

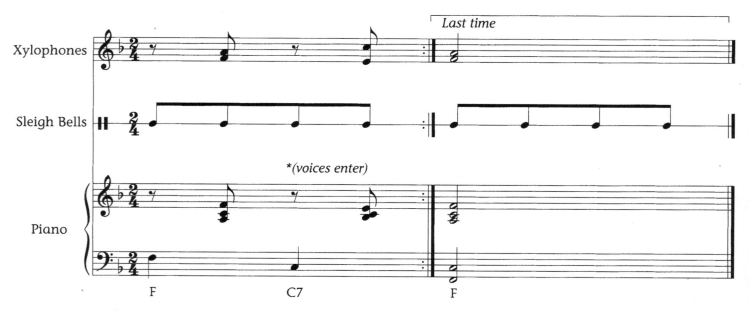

*NOTE: Use two bars introduction, the VOICES entering on the *second* half of the *second* bar.

Let In The Spring
(Three part round)

Performance Accomp.

Words and Music by
Eileen Diamond

Not too fast

O - pen the win - dow and hear the birds sing,

No - tice how blos - soms round the trees cling,

O - pen the win - dow, let in the Spring.

Accompaniment Ostinato

Let in the Spring.

Gm   D   D7   Gm

Musical Feelings

Words and Music by
Eileen Diamond

1. I have a musical feeling
   And I'll play it on the piano.
   I have a musical feeling,
   Listen while I play it for you now.

2. James has a musical feeling
   And he'll play it on the piano.
   James has a musical feeling,
   Listen while he plays it for us now.

   etc.

TEACHING IDEAS

A song incorporating the skills of listening, appraising, improvisation, creativity, rhythm and musical imagination.

Performance

The teacher sings the first verse and improvises a 'Musical feeling' at the end. Alternatively, the children may sing the verse using the teachers name.

Miss/Mr/Mrs has a musical feeling and she/he'll play it etc.

Adapt the rhythm to fit different names.

The children then take it in turns to improvise a 'Musical feeling' after the verse has been sung using the child's name.

Any tuned instruments may be used that the children are familiar with: piano, xylophone, metallophone, recorder, violin, guitar etc.

Further discussion and development ideas

Discuss the 'Musical feeling' after it has been played.

Was it happy or sad? Fast or slow? Loud or quiet? Jumpy (staccato) or smooth (legato)? etc. Could they clap the rhythm or sing any part of the melody?

A Sound Round
(Four part round)

Words and Music by
Eileen Diamond

Briskly

① Doo doo doo doo doo, doo doo doo, doo doo doo.

② La la la la la, la la la la la la la la.

③ Aah aah aah, aah aah aah.

④ Pom pom pom pom pom, pom pom pom pom.

Accompaniment Ostinato

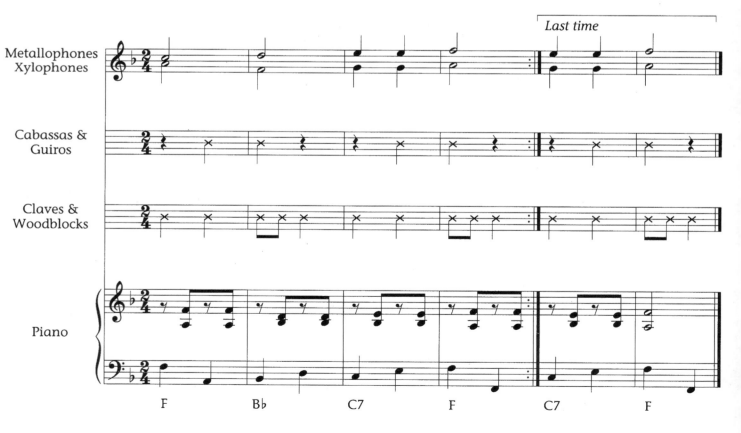

Metallophones Xylophones

Cabassas & Guiros

Claves & Woodblocks

Piano

F   B♭   C7   F   C7   F

TEACHING IDEAS

A four part round with an instrumental ostinato.

Performance

First learn the round in unison, until it is quite secure. Practise each instrumental part on its own before playing them together.

Remember to decide how many times to perform the round before you start!

Try the following performance suggestion:

1. The piano plays the 4 bar ostinato once.

2. The metallophone and xylophones join in for 4 more bars.

3. The guiros and cabassas join them for 4 bars.

4. The claves and wood blocks join them for 4 more bars.

The ostinato continues while the round is sung once in unison, then three times through in parts.

The round may also be sung unaccompanied, or with percussion only or piano only accompaniment.

Further discussion and development ideas

This round would work with any vocal sounds and once it is known, the children may like to suggest some other sounds to sing and experiment with the different textures they produce.

This could be done in groups, with each group composing and performing their own sounds and listening to and appraising the others.

Who Likes The Winter?

Words and Music by
Eileen Diamond

Why does it come? When will it go?

Who likes the win — — ter? Why must it stay?

Hur — ry up spring-time, send win ter a - way! - way!

Frost in the air, snow on the hills,
Icicles hanging from window sills.
Cloudy and grey, day after day,
Unwelcome winter, why must you stay?

Who likes the winter? Who likes the snow?
Why does it come? When will it go?
Who likes the winter? Why must it stay?
Hurry up springtime, send winter away!

Who likes the winter? Who likes the snow? etc.

TEACHING IDEAS

A song to tie in with seasonal and weather topics, using percussion instruments to create special effects.

INSTRUMENTS: TAMBOURINES, INDIAN BELLS, TRIANGLES, DRUMS, CLAVES, XYLOPHONES, GLOCKENSPIELS.

XYLOPHONES AND GLOCKENSPIELS require notes G, A, B, D only, others may be removed.

Tambourine: shake 〰〰〰〰 tap ↓

Triangle: play rapidly (tremolo) 〰〰〰〰 strike ↓

Performance

When the song has been learnt, practise the instrumental parts separately.

Note the xylophone/glockenspiel pattern:

E, A, A, B, G, A, A played 3 times. Then last time: E, A, A, B, A, A, D

Keep the drum beats gentle on the words 'Cloudy and grey' and a little stronger in the second part of the song where they play on the 1st beat of the bar (followed by the claves).

Notice the different rhythmic patterns when all percussion play.

Further discussion and development ideas

This song illustrates the cold, unwelcoming side of winter, but children often enjoy the snow. Discuss the pros and cons of winter and summer and the different activities that go with each. Take a vote on which they prefer.

Exercises

Words and Music by
Eileen Diamond

Lively

VERSE

If you want to keep your bo-dy heal-thy, vig-or-ous, strong and fit, There is
some-thing you must re-al-ize, The ma-gic word is EX-ER-CISE, Just a
lit-tle ev-ery-day, You can do it this way...

CHORUS

Verse
If you want to keep your body healthy, vigorous, strong and fit,
There is something you must realize,
The magic word is EXERCISE,
Just a little everyday,
You can do it this way . . .

Chorus

Group One
Stretch up high, high, high,when you're doing your exercises.

Group Two
Loosen up, loosen up, everybody loosen up, doing your exercises.

Group Three
Bend your elbows, bend your elbows, doing your exercises.

TEACHING IDEAS

A health and fitness song! The verse is sung in unison, followed by an accumulative type of chorus building up into three parts, each with its own exercise to perform!

Performance

First divide the voices into three groups and teach each group its CHORUS and its exercise. Then, when secure:

1. All sing the VERSE, then GROUP 1 Sing their CHORUS twice and perform their actions at the same time.

2. All sing the VERSE, then GROUP 2 sing their CHORUS twice (alone) then twice more joined by GROUP 1.

3. All sing the VERSE, then GROUP 3 sing their CHORUS twice (alone) then twice more joined by GROUP 2 and then both groups continue joined by GROUP 1. At the end, the choruses may be repeated any pre-arranged number of times.

GROUP 1	EXERCISES
Stretch up high	stretch arms straight up
High, high	sway arms right, then left
When you're doing your exercises	sway right, then left, then straight up and bring arms down Repeat as necessary

GROUP 2

Shake wrists

GROUP 3

Bend elbows, push arms out in front and back again

Roundabouts
(Two part round)

Words and Music by
Eileen Diamond

Brightly

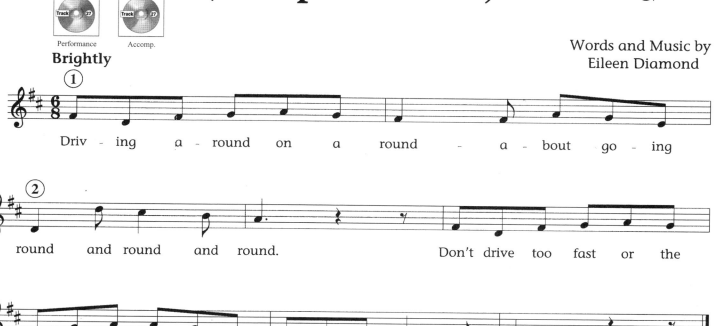

Driv - ing a - round on a round - a - bout go - ing round and round and round. Don't drive too fast or the ex - it you'll pass and you'll keep go - ing round and round.

Accompaniment Ostinato

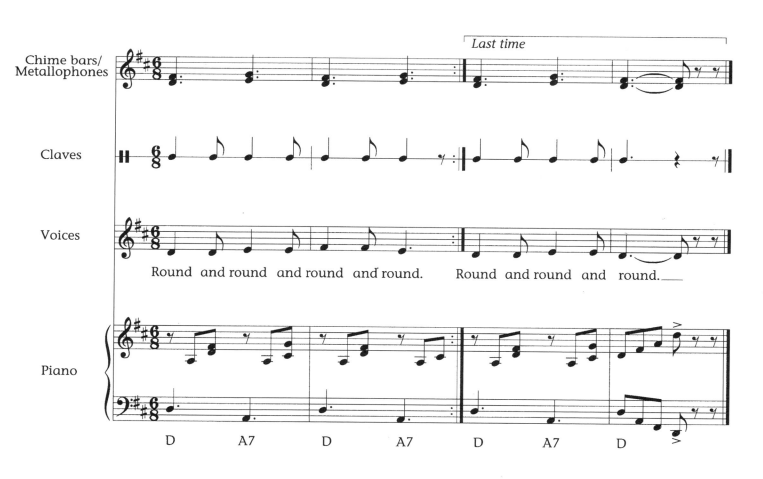

Round and round and round and round. Round and round and round.

Notes

Notes